SNAKE in THE GRASS

" . . . a terrific piece - brilliant, bizarre and yet totally believable." *Yorkshire Post*

" . . . subtle and powerful . . . " *Guardian*

"I defy anyone to write for women as well as Sir Alan . . ." *Teletext*

" . . . nobody structures a play with more perfect control of his craft . . ." *What's On Stage*

Snake in the Grass

A play

Alan Ayckbourn

Samuel French — London
New York · Toronto · Hollywood

SNAKE IN THE GRASS

First performed at the Stephen Joseph Theatre, Scarborough, on 5th June 2002, with the following cast:

Annabel Chester   Fiona Mollison
Alice Moody   Rachel Atkins
Miriam Chester   Susie Blake

Directed by **Alan Ayckbourn**
Designed by **Roger Glossop**
Lighting designed by **Mick Hughes**
Costumes designed by **Christine Wall**
Music by **John Pattison**

CHARACTERS

Annabel Chester, 50
Miriam Chester, Annabel's younger sister, 44
Alice Moody, a nurse, 40s

The action of the play takes place in the garden of the Chesters' house

ACT I

ACT II

Plays by Alan Ayckbourn published by Samuel French Ltd

ACT I

A garden. Late afternoon in August

We see part of a tennis court which, although in evident disrepair, has solid enough fencing and a door that is in working order. The rest of the court extends off stage. There is a bench alongside the court. At the other side, a small summer-house/pavilion, very weathered and derelict. This contains a solitary piece of furniture, an old, weather-worn, but solid and still serviceable rocking chair. There is a practical trap-door concealing a well. From the roof hangs a rusty outdoor wind chime. It is far too calm a day, though, for this to sound

Elsewhere, rough grass underfoot. Bushes and trees

Annabel, a rather gaunt, tense, middle-aged woman is standing staring round the garden. Despite the bright afternoon sunshine, the cheerful birdsong and the general air of peace and tranquillity, her memories of this place appear to be disturbing ones. She moves to the summer-house and can't resist brushing the wind chime with her finger. It chimes sweetly. But does little to reassure her

Alice enters

Annabel doesn't see her at first. Alice studies her

Alice *(eventually, with a slight Northern accent)* Mrs Morton?
Annabel *(starting slightly)* Oh! *(Seeing Alice at last, slightly abruptly)* Yes?
Alice Alice Moody.
Annabel Oh, yes?
Alice You'll be Mrs Morton?
Annabel No. I was.
Alice Ah.
Annabel Not any more.
Alice Oh.
Annabel I'm Annabel Chester.
Alice How do you do.

Annabel Who did you say you were?

Alice Alice Moody.

Annabel Do I know you?

Alice I'm——

Annabel Ought I to know you?

Alice I'm—I was your father's nurse. At one time. I don't know if your sister mentioned me at all…?

Annabel Oh, yes. Alice. Of course. Yes. Miriam did mention you. In her letters. Yes. Alice Moody?

Alice That's right.

Annabel Yes. (*A slight pause*) Alice *Moody*. Just a moment, aren't you the one my sister got rid of?

Alice Technically speaking, yes.

Annabel Hardly technically. She fired you, didn't she?

Alice She chose to dispense with my nursing services, yes.

Annabel Then what are you still doing here?

Alice I needed to have a——

Annabel Not back to nurse my father, I trust?

Alice No, of course not, I was——

Annabel Because I've bad news if you have, he died three weeks ago. (*She laughs. Annabel's humour is an acquired taste*)

Alice Yes, I'm well aware that your father's deceased, Miss Chester.

Annabel Then why are you here? If my sister got rid of you, there was obviously——

Alice If you'd allow me to explain, Miss Chester, I——

Annabel Where is my sister, anyway? I arrive to find the house all locked up. Where's Miriam?

Alice I believe she's presently at the shops.

Annabel The shops?

Alice Shopping. She doesn't know I'm here, you see.

Annabel She doesn't?

Alice No, I came to see you, Miss Chester.

Annabel Me?

Alice It's a delicate matter. I needed to speak to you privately.

Annabel How did you know I'd even be here?

Alice I was—I was aware you would be…

Annabel Did you now? I've only just got off the plane and here you are lying in wait for me.

Alice I knew you'd be home sooner or later, Miss Chester. I was familiar with the terms of your father's final will, you see. I felt certain you'd be here.

Annabel How do you know about my father's will? Who told you about that?

Alice Your father and I became quite close friends by the end, before I was—forced to leave.

Annabel Did you?

Alice I rather expected to see you here for the funeral, as a matter of fact.

Annabel Did you? Well, I wasn't.

Alice Seeing it was your own father's.

Annabel What exactly do you want, Miss Moody?

Alice I've said. I'd like a word with you, Miss Chester, if I may.

Annabel If you're claiming you were wrongfully dismissed or somesuch, I should take it up with the Royal College of Nursing or whatever...

Alice *(calmly)* No, it's not about that.

Annabel ...because there is no point in talking to me about it. If I remember correctly, according to my sister, she dismissed you because you were unpunctual, neglectful, unreliable and unprofessional.

Alice Is that what she called me?

Annabel So far as I remember. I may have them in the wrong order and there may have been a few more reasons, I can't recall. Now I suggest you leave at once, please.

Alice I don't know why you're being quite so hostile, Miss Chester.

Annabel Because I've had an extremely long flight, I'm very jet-lagged and from what I've learnt from my sister you're not someone whom she'd particularly welcome in her garden, Miss Moody.

Alice Your garden.

Annabel What?

Alice Your garden, surely? I understood this garden belongs to you now. Since your father's departure. Surely?

Annabel What business is that of yours?

Alice I mean, if we're being strictly accurate—technically—I understood that under the terms of the will you own, or will shortly own, the house, this garden and all the contents.

Annabel Possibly. What of it?

Alice Plus the bulk of the estate.

Annabel I don't know how you obtained this information...

Alice I obtained it because your father wrote to me and told me that was what he was doing.

Annabel He did?

Alice Altering his will. In your favour. Just a few days before he died.

Annabel I see.

Alice But that's not all he wrote to tell me. He also wrote to say he was almost certain your sister was trying to kill him.

Pause

Annabel I beg your pardon?

Alice That's what he believed.

Annabel What rubbish!

Alice I've got the letter.

Annabel This is complete nonsense. *Miriam?* My sister *Miriam?*

Alice Would you care to see it? (*She produces a sheet of paper from her bag*) Here. It's all right, you can keep it. It's a photocopy. (*She hands the paper to Annabel*)

After a second, Annabel takes it and starts to read it. Alice watches her

I have shown the original to your sister. It's perfectly genuine, isn't it? Definitely your father's handwriting. A little bit shaky, but then he was very ill. He must have dragged himself all the way to the post box. On his own. While your sister was out. That must have taken a bit of doing. He was very weak, even when I was still here to care for him. After I went, with the dosages your sister was giving him, God knows what sort of state he must have been in. Amazing he could stand up at all, really.

Annabel (*finishing the letter*) This is no sort of proof at all.

Alice No? Don't you think so?

Annabel This is clearly written by a man who hardly knew what he was doing. He was probably not even thinking straight. Look at the state of the handwriting. He was obviously delirious. Fantasizing.

Alice Oh, but he wasn't, you see.

Annabel How do you know? You weren't even here.

Alice I know because when I confronted your sister with it a few days ago, she admitted it.

Annabel Admitted what?

Alice That ... she'd been doubling his doses. Tripling them some days.

Annabel She admitted it?

Alice Evidently one night he got up to answer a call of nature, hardly knowing where he was at all, blundering about in the dark—he wandered on to the landing looking for the—little boys' room—and she shoved him down the stairs.

Annabel She pushed him?

Alice The poor man never stood a chance. It was pitch dark, you see. She'd taken all the light bulbs out as well, just to make sure.

Annabel This is unbelievable. I'm sorry. I simply do not believe you. You're talking about my sister Miriam. She would never do anything like that to a living soul. Let alone her own father. She's—she's the gentlest, most— harmless person in the world...

Alice You haven't seen her for a bit, though, have you?

Annabel No. But we've corresponded regularly. I——

Alice I think you might be a little bit surprised when you see her. She's probably changed a lot since you last saw her. Someone who spends fifteen years of their life, virtually a prisoner, looking after a sick old man—no social life to speak of—no—sex life—no nothing—well, you might undergo a few changes yourself. But you were all right, weren't you? Safe and sound in Australia.

Annabel Tasmania, if you must know.

Alice Well out of it there, weren't you?

Annabel That is absolutely none of your business.

Pause

If you must know, my father and I—never saw eye to eye.

Alice I see.

Annabel I was forced to stay away. We simply didn't agree on things.

Alice He liked you enough to leave you everything, anyway.

Annabel Well. People do that. When people realize they're dying they often—want to try and put things straight, don't they? That's all that was.

Alice Just in case, eh?

Annabel If you like.

Pause

Anyway, assuming there's a single grain of truth in all this——

Alice Oh, there's more than a grain, believe me——

Annabel —what do you hope to get out of it?

Alice Why should I want anything?

Annabel Obviously you do. Or you'd have done your proper duty as a nurse and reported all this in the first place.

Alice Yes, I probably should have done that.

Annabel Then don't stand there pretending you don't want anything.

Alice I'm not pretending.

Annabel Well, then.

Alice I want a considerable amount, as a matter of fact, Miss Chester. I think I'm entitled to that for wrongful dismissal, don't you? Despite what your sister said to you, I was a good nurse to your father. I was very fond of him and all—he was a wicked old boy, he used to make me laugh like a drain— and I took good care of him. Too much care, as it happens. If I'd been working here now, he'd have still been alive, wouldn't he? Only your sister chose to get shot of me in order that she could get rid of him. Calling me incompetent. Tarnishing my professional reputation. I think I'm entitled to something for that, don't you?

Pause

Annabel I see. What is it you want, then?

Alice I've already told your sister what I want.

Annabel Then why are you talking to me?

Alice Because I thought, as her sister, you ought to be aware of the situation. And I wasn't sure how much she'd tell you.

Annabel I see.

Alice Besides, I thought the least you were entitled to was the truth, seeing as you're the one who now has all the money.

Annabel Ah.

Alice No point in asking her for anything. Poor cow hasn't even got a decent coat to her back.

Annabel Would you kindly not refer to my sister like that!

Alice I have to say he kept her on a short chain, your father. Just enough to get her to the village shop and back. Hardly what you'd call a generous allowance…

Annabel Now you listen to me. I want you to leave now, do you hear? I will talk to my sister——

Alice Yes, you'll need to talk to her——

Annabel —I say, I will talk to my sister and get to the bottom of all this. But I must tell you that my instinct at present, Miss Moody, is to call the police and have you charged with extortion and blackmail.

Alice You could give it a go if you like. It'll all have to come out then, won't it? Depends how much you care for your sister, I suppose. Tell you what, I'll come back tomorrow around about this same time, shall I? Then we can all sit down and discuss it properly. I'll leave you a night to sleep on it. Get over your jet lag.

Annabel You will come back when we call you back.

Alice You don't know where I live though, these days, do you? But I know where you live. Good afternoon, Miss Chester. Or may I call you Annabel?

Annabel You most certainly may not. Good afternoon, Miss Moody.

Alice (*imperviously*) I'll go out the back way. I'll see you later.

Alice goes out past the tennis court

Annabel stands for a moment

Annabel (*shaking her head in disbelief, to herself*) Oh, my God. Miriam!

Suddenly, the mesh of the tennis court fencing resonates as if something or someone has knocked against it

(*Startled; calling*) Who's that?

No reply

Who's there? Is there someone there?

Miriam, her younger sister, appears at the mesh. In contrast with Annabel she is a rounded, soft, rather vulnerable figure

Miriam (*rather tearful*) Annabel...?
Annabel (*only half recognizing her*) Miriam...?

Miriam comes out of the court and embraces Annabel passionately

Miriam Oh, Annie, it's good to see you! I'm so glad you're here!
Annabel (*rather taken aback by this effusiveness*) Miriam, what are you doing? How long have you been there?
Miriam I came back from the village—I saw you talking to her—I just had to hide. (*She goes totally to pieces*) Oh, Annie, she's a terrible woman— you've no idea ... it's been a nightmare, it's just been a nightmare...
Annabel Miriam! Miriam, calm down, now. Just calm down. My God, woman, look at you. Look at the state of you...
Miriam I'm sorry. I'm sorry. I'm such a mess.
Annabel Sit down, now. Come along. Sit down. (*She seats Miriam on the bench*)
Miriam I'm such a terrible mess. Oh, Annie, I'm so happy to see you, you've no idea...
Annabel Miriam, is all this true? All the things that woman's told me? Are they really true?
Miriam Oh, God! I'm such a mess...
Annabel Miriam...
Miriam ...such an awful mess...
Annabel Yes, I can see you are.
Miriam ...just look at me...
Annabel Yes, I've looked, I've said. Now, Miriam, what that woman told me just now—is any of it true? Is there any truth in it?
Miriam You don't know what it was like, Annie, those last months, you don't know. He was getting worse and worse.
Annabel Father?
Miriam He was just terrible to me. So cruel and unkind, I couldn't do anything right for him... (*She weeps afresh*) Everything I did, he ... he shouted ... and threw things and threw his food... I just couldn't take any more...
Annabel Miriam, calmly now. Calm down, dear. Take a few breaths.

Miriam does this

That's it. Deep breaths.

Miriam (*a little calmer*) Sorry. I'm sorry. God, I'm such a mess.

Annabel Yes, yes, we've established that. (*She finds a tissue*) Here... Wipe yourself a bit.

Miriam Thank you... I'm sorry... I never even asked. How are you? Did you have a good flight?

Annabel Yes, I had a perfectly wonderful flight. Apart from being seated next to a woman with a screaming baby all the way from Singapore, absolutely perfect—now never mind about me. Miriam, tell me something. I need to know. How much of our conversation, me and that woman's, did you hear just now?

Miriam (*snuffling*) A little bit, just a little bit...

Annabel (*talking to her like a child*) Then tell me, honestly. Now you have to be honest with me, Miriam ... do you hear me? Honest?

Miriam (*weakly*) Yes.

Annabel Promise?

Miriam Yes...

Annabel Tell me, did you deliberately dismiss that woman?

Miriam Yes.

Annabel Why?

A little wail from Miriam

Don't start again! That isn't helpful.

Miriam Sorry.

Annabel Did you dismiss her so that you could start—altering father's medicine?

Another wail

Miriam, was that the reason? Was it or wasn't it?

Miriam (*faintly*) Yes...

Annabel Did you deliberately increase his dosage?

Miriam (*nodding*) A little bit...

Annabel A little bit?

Miriam I thought it might make him sleep more. So he wouldn't shout at me.

Annabel What do you mean by a little bit?

Miriam shakes her head

Did you double the dose?

Miriam shakes her head again

Triple the dose?

Miriam Maybe a little bit more.

Annabel Oh, God in heaven! And did you really push him down the stairs?

Miriam Only a little push...

Annabel (*agitatedly moving from her*) Oh, dear Lord! Oh, dear heavens! And did you also remove the light bulbs as well...?

Miriam Just one or two...

Annabel Miriam! You murdered him. You murdered Father. Do you understand that?

Miriam I didn't mean to...

Annabel What do you mean, you didn't mean to?

Miriam It was an accident...

Annabel Miriam, I've never heard anything less like an accident... You deliberately give him quadruple doses of medicine, you take out all the light bulbs and push him down the stairs... No-one in the world's going to believe that was an accident, Miriam, are they?

Miriam starts crying afresh

And you've confessed all that to this woman?

Miriam She had the letter. She showed me the letter from Father.

Annabel I see. And it seemed perfectly genuine to you?

Miriam Oh, yes... It was on his writing paper...

Annabel Yes, well, that's not necessarily—And what did she say to you?

Miriam She said unless we—you gave her an awful lot of money she'd show the letter to the authorities—and then they—they'd dig up Daddy and have a post...

Annabel A post? You mean an autopsy?

Miriam Yes.

Annabel Would they be able to tell, after all this time?

Miriam Oh, yes. She's a nurse, she said they'd be able to tell, once they started looking for it... Then I'd have to go to prison. I don't want to go to prison, Annie...

Annabel Don't be silly. You wouldn't go to prison...

Miriam She said I would.

Annabel She's just trying to frighten you, that's all... You're not going to go to prison...

Miriam You just said I deliberately murdered Father. Don't they send you to prison for that? For deliberately murdering your father.

Annabel Yes, well—sometimes maybe they probably do, yes. Sometimes. It depends if there are any extenuating... (*She gives this up*) Listen, Miriam, what does she want from us, that woman? Did she tell you what she wanted in order to keep quiet?

Miriam Yes.

Annabel Money, she wanted money, you say?

Miriam Yes.
Annabel How much money, Miriam?

Miriam hesitates

Miriam, how much does she want?
Miriam A hundred thousand pounds.

Silence. Even the birds have stopped singing

Annabel (*at last*) I don't have a hundred thousand pounds. I don't have that
   much money in the world.
Miriam You don't?
Annabel Of course I don't. Not at all. I have practically nothing left of my
   own. A tiny little bit set aside to live on. Invested. A few stocks and shares,
   that's it. I don't have that sort of money.
Miriam What are we going to do then? What am I going to do? What do we
   say to her?
Annabel We'll tell her she's—she's going to have to whistle for it. We
   simply don't have it.
Miriam What about from your business?
Annabel Miriam, I wrote and told you my business folded. You know it did.
Miriam Oh, yes.
Annabel I no longer have a business, any more than I still have a husband,
   thank God. Practically all I have in the world is in those three suitcases
   outside the back door there.
Miriam Then what am I going to do?
Annabel I don't know. I really don't.
Miriam If we don't pay her what she wants, she'll go to the police.
Annabel Then she'll have to. She needs to understand we simply cannot pay
   her that sort of money.
Miriam What about what Father left you?
Annabel According to the lawyer's letter, that amounts to considerably less
   than a hundred thousand pounds, I can promise you that. And after death
   duties…
Miriam What about the house?
Annabel Yes, I planned to sell this, anyway. But we'll need that money in
   order to buy somewhere else for ourselves, won't we? Somewhere
   smaller. For us both. In, say, Fulham perhaps. I rather fancied Fulham.
Miriam Fulham?
Annabel Well, somewhere—like Fulham. I don't know. Something with
   two bedrooms, you know. Nothing too grand but… With both of us
   working—we should just about manage. I had it all planned out. I can go

back to secretarial work—temporarily. Until I find something more challenging.

Miriam You're all right to work again, now?

Annabel Oh yes, of course I am. Providing I'm sensible. I'm perfectly fit.

Miriam What about me, then? What shall I do? If I'm not in prison?

Annabel You? Well, you can—you can—we'll find you something, don't worry… You can go back to teaching, surely?

Miriam I haven't been in a classroom for ten years——

Annabel That doesn't matter—the children aren't going to know the difference. Most of them are so stupid these days, anyway. And besides, you were a drama teacher, weren't you? That's not going to have changed. It'll be the same old waving and shouting, surely? (*She laughs. It's another of her jokes*)

Miriam (*gloomily*) What am I going to do, Annie? Seriously…

Annabel Oh, come on, Miriam. We'll sort it out, don't worry. At least if you go to prison that'll save us some money, anyway. (*She laughs again*) No, the point is we're not giving that woman a hundred thousand pounds, I can tell you that. Even if I had it, that would go completely against the grain.

Miriam Then I will go to prison.

Annabel Listen, we'll meet her here tomorrow afternoon as she suggests and I'll offer her—a—a compromise sum. I'll have to do some calculations this evening to see how much I can afford to give her. And she'll have to be content with that, won't she?

Miriam What if she isn't?

Annabel She'll have to be. She won't get any more. There'll certainly be no negotiation.

Miriam But what if she—says no?

Annabel That won't happen.

Miriam You don't know her. You don't know Alice.

Annabel Then we'll—we'll face that if it comes, won't we? Come on, I'm desperate for a cup of tea. Then I need to go to bed and sleep. I'll unpack in the morning. I hope you've given me my old room?

Miriam Yes. I'm afraid it's all a bit—run down, though…

Annabel It certainly looks it from the outside. When on earth was it last painted?

Miriam Oh, God knows… Not in my lifetime…

Annabel (*moving off*) Come along, Miriam, brighten up now. We'll think of something, don't worry. We're bound to think of something, aren't we?

Annabel strides off towards the house

Miriam (*following her*) Yes, we're sure to think of something.

As Miriam goes the Lights fade to Black-out

The same. The following afternoon

Again, it is very warm and sunny

*Annabel is waiting. She again seems to be drawn towards the tennis court.
She stares through the fence*

*In a moment, Miriam enters with a small folding table and an upright garden
chair*

*She goes to the summer-house and during the following sets up the table in
front of the rocking chair and then positions the garden chair. The atmosphere
seems a little cooler between the two women*

Annabel (*watching Miriam*) I don't know why we're bothering with this, I
really don't.

Miriam does not reply

We're treating the woman like some honoured guest.
Miriam (*coolly*) No, we're not.
Annabel It's all cut and dried. I've been over all my accounts this morning.
I'm offering her five thousand and that's it. She can take it or leave it. No
negotiation. Nothing. That is final.
Miriam Yes, you said.
Annabel That's all I can afford. And I have to say yet again, I begrudge every
penny.
Miriam And if she refuses to accept that?
Annabel Too bad. That's all. Too bad.

Miriam is silent

Frankly, Miriam, I don't believe that we have that many other options. If
she refuses to accept the five thousand—and I'm fully prepared to give her
cash in hand—if she refuses—then the chances are, if she's the type of
woman you say she is, that she will go to the police and show them Father's
letter. And should they choose to follow it up, which I presume they will,
then they will probably exhume Father's body—why on earth you didn't
have him cremated…
Miriam He didn't want to be. He didn't like it.
Annabel Right—they will probably exhume Father's body and, if she's

right and they do detect evidence of the overdose—then that will establish a *prima facie* case and the result of that will be—that you'll probably be arrested, prosecuted and go to prison for a considerable time. I mean, that's it in a nutshell.

Silence

Miriam That's your alternative scheme, is it?

Annabel As I see it. I'm sorry, Miriam, but you really have behaved extremely stupidly. I mean, I have every sympathy with you pushing Father downstairs—I'd probably have done much the same in your place—but to involve a woman like that and then to confess it all to her...

Miriam (*starting to walk towards the house; quietly*) All right. (*She appears to have come to some sort of decision*)

Annabel Where are you going now?

Miriam I'm fetching some wine.

Annabel Wine? We're offering that woman wine?

Miriam We can at least try to get her an our side, can't we?

Annabel Listen, all I'm offering is the money and saying, take it or leave it. That's it. Goodbye. This is not a social occasion. It's bad enough offering her a chair——

Miriam (*angrily*) Look, it's all right for you, isn't it? I'm the one that has to——

Annabel (*responding*) What do you mean, it's all right for me?

Miriam —I'm the one that has to——

Annabel —it is certainly not all right for me——

Miriam (*shouting*)—I'm the one that has to go to prison if she refuses to——

Annabel (*shouting*)—and I'm the one who has to find all the money in the first place, aren't I?

Silence. They stand glaring at each other

Miriam (*calming down*) We're arguing again.

Annabel Well. Honestly.

Miriam That's the third argument we've had since you came back.

Annabel (*dryly*) Really?

Miriam You've only been back a day.

Annabel Well, you're an extremely irritating person sometimes.

Miriam First you were on about your bedroom curtains...

Annabel They clash with the bedspread. What was wrong with the old ones?

Miriam They were forty years old and falling to pieces——

Annabel Because they'd been hand washed. I told you, if they'd been properly dry cleaned like they were supposed to be——

Miriam (*shouting*) Don't start again!

Silence

Annabel (*muttering*) They'd have lasted a lifetime.

Slight pause

What was the other one, anyway?

Miriam (*through clenched teeth*) I'd bought the wrong-sized eggs for breakfast. Need I say more? I rest my case.

Annabel I've told you, they're too much for me, I can't eat large eggs.

Miriam (*muttering*) I don't know why not. Your mouth's big enough.

Annabel What?

Miriam I'll fetch the wine.

Miriam goes off to the house

Annabel (*calling after her*) Not for me! (*She mutters to herself*) Wasting wine on that—woman. (*She stands looking around her*) I can't possibly eat large eggs. They don't even taste the same. They put something in them, I know they do. (*She moves to the tennis court and presses her face to the mesh fence. Quite suddenly she gives a little cry, half in anguish, half in pain. She clutches her chest and moves with difficulty to retrieve her handbag. She takes out a strip of tablets, pops two out of their foil and swallows them. She sits in one of the chairs to recover, trying to control her breathing*)

Miriam returns with a tray with a bottle of quite decent white wine already opened and three glasses. It appears that Miriam has already poured herself a glass. The bottle is depleted and one of the glasses is already filled

Miriam (*putting the tray on the table*) What's left from the cellar. Might as well use it up. Father never got round to it. (*She notices Annabel*) You all right?

Annabel Yes, just a—I'm fine.

Miriam Another one?

Annabel Just a mild one… It's not serious.

Miriam You had one this morning.

Annabel It's not a problem. It's probably still the jet lag.

Miriam You should see someone.

Annabel I already have. I know what it is, I have the medication and it's not a problem. Now forget it. Is one of those glasses intended for me?

Miriam Yes, I thought you might like a——
Annabel I told you, I don't. I told you that. Not any more.
Miriam I thought maybe a small one…
Annabel Miriam, if you're someone like me, there's no such thing as a small drink. It's all or nothing.
Miriam Right. (*She takes her own glass and sips it*)
Annabel And you'd better watch it, as well.
Miriam How do you mean?
Annabel You were knocking them back last night, too, weren't you?
Miriam I may have had a glass or two. It was only wine.
Annabel Hah! Only wine, she says.
Miriam God, is there anything more boring than a reformed alcoholic?
Annabel I know what I'm talking about, that's all——
Miriam A born again non-smoker, perhaps?
Annabel I've never smoked.
Miriam Thank God for that! We'd never have heard the end of it.

Pause

We never got on, did we? Even in the early days. You were always shouting at me. My big sister. You were meant to take care of me. All you ever did was shout at me. Or ignore me completely when it suited you.
Annabel You were a spoilt little brat. Daddy's little girl.
Miriam Some days you'd look straight through me. Like I wasn't even there.
Annabel You were also a congenital liar and extremely irritating…
Miriam Maybe I was just trying to get some attention…
Annabel Well, you succeeded.

Pause

By the way, you haven't changed a bit, you're still extremely irritating…
Miriam Thank you so much.

Pause

Annabel I'm sorry. That wasn't very nice.
Miriam It wasn't.
Annabel I'm sorry.

Pause

Miriam You just say things, don't you? You just say things without thinking sometimes, don't you? So clever. And yet so hurtful. Born with all the brains and you never even bother to think half the time.

Annabel Maybe you're right. Don't worry, I've paid for it in my time. Don't worry.

Miriam Then perhaps you should have learnt from experience.

Annabel Do we ever? Any of us? We're what we are, aren't we? I'm thoughtless and you're stupid.

Miriam There you go again!

Annabel I'm sorry. And I'm sorry if I gave you a rotten childhood. I had a pretty rotten one myself...

Miriam I'm sure you did. I know you did. Some of it, anyway. From what I can remember—what I could understand of it.

Slight pause

Nevertheless, it was extremely hurtful to me. That's all I'm saying. When Mother died it was so lonely. Once you'd gone—run off. Just me, Father and Auntie Gwen...

Annabel Auntie Gwen. My God. It's amazing you survived at all, really. (*She laughs, one of her laughs*) It's certainly amazing you have anything left to drink in the wine cellar, anyway.

Miriam Auntie Gwen only drank vodka.

Annabel So she did.

Miriam Lots and lots of vodka. I needed a big sister. You should have been here, Annabel. You shouldn't have gone away.

Annabel Well, I couldn't stay. And I've told you before, don't call me Annabel. Annie or Anna if you have to, please.

Miriam Sorry!

Annabel The only person who called me Annabel was Father.

Miriam How could I forget? The last few days that was practically all he said. Annabel, Annabel! Where's Annabel? Go away, you, I want Annabel! Annabel, Annabel, Annabel!

Annabel I don't believe that.

Miriam She's not here, you stupid man. She ran off thirty-five years ago.

Slight pause

It's true.

Annabel Well, don't call me it again, please.

Miriam I'll try and remember.

Annabel It always makes me feel I've done something terribly wrong.

Miriam finishes her wine and immediately pours herself another from the bottle

You're not having another one, surely?

Miriam Just a minute. I'll fetch the other chair. She should be here soon. (*She walks back towards the house, carrying her glass. She pauses and looks back at Annabel*) That summer-house hasn't been used for years, you know. When you're on your own you don't really bother, do you?

Annabel I can't remember us ever using it, actually. He only had it built because of the well, didn't he?

Miriam Oh yes, the well. I'd forgotten the well.

Annabel To stop either of us falling down it. Is it still there?

Miriam Probably. The trap-door is, certainly.

Annabel Where?

Miriam Where you're sitting, I think.

Annabel (*rising hastily*) Oh, yes.

Miriam It's OK. It hasn't been opened for years. (*She starts to go*) Won't be a second.

Miriam goes back to the house

Annabel picks up the bottle and examines the label and the contents. She frowns and puts down the bottle. Suddenly the tennis court fencing gives another twang as if something or someone has knocked against it. Annabel starts rather nervously

Annabel (*approaching the court; cautiously*) Who's that? Is someone there? (*She listens*) Who is that? Miss Moody? I can see you, you know.

Pause

Hallo?

Miriam enters with her glass and carrying a second folding chair

Miriam What's wrong?

Annabel I think there's someone in there.

Miriam (*putting down the chair and joining her*) Where?

Annabel I heard them just now. Banging against the fencing.

Miriam (*looking through the mesh*) Well, there's no-one in there now. God, it's overgrown. Couldn't play in here now, could you?

Annabel Even if you wanted to. Maybe they're round the side. Look round the side.

Miriam investigates

Anything?

Miriam Not a soul.

Annabel I heard something.

Miriam Probably a bird. They're always flying into that fence. Stupid things. (*She returns to the chair and puts it up*)

Annabel stays by the court

Annabel I've always hated this place.

Miriam What, the tennis court?

Annabel Don't you remember? No, you would have been too young. I was seven, eight years old. Every single day of the holidays. When I wasn't trapped in that bloody awful boarding school. He used to drag me out here each afternoon, determined to teach me.

Miriam Father did?

Annabel God, he was relentless. Come along, Annabel. Hit it, girl! Hit the damn thing! What's the matter with you, girl? Firing these bloody tennis balls at me, hour after hour, ball after ball. In the end I was crying so much, I could no longer see them anyway. Faster and faster—used to hit me, a lot of them. Couldn't get out of the way quick enough. But then he was—so strong. And I was always, a little—uncoordinated. Like human target practice. Black and blue. Come on, Annabel, shift your fat arse! I used to fall over, my knees were skinned, my elbows were grazed... It suddenly all came back to me just now. God, how I loathe sport. I could never watch Wimbledon.

Miriam (*sipping her wine*) Still, it's a lovely garden. I'll miss it. If we move to Fulham.

Annabel I only said—Fulham. Could be somewhere else. Battersea, even.

Miriam Ah. (*She reflects*) Couldn't we just stay here?

Annabel I don't want to stay here. It's full of the most awful memories. Isn't it for you? It must be.

Miriam Well... It's just I've lived here for ever, that's all.

Annabel Time for a change, then, surely. Anyway. There's no work round here. We'd both have to commute. We can't start all that at our age.

Miriam A lot of people do.

Annabel Well, I'm not one of them. (*She looks at Miriam with displeasure*) Do you drink a lot on your own?

Miriam Oh, don't get at me again!

Annabel No, do you? I'm asking.

Miriam I have the occasional glass, yes. In the evening. Why not? I think I'm entitled to some pleasures.

Annabel Fine. Do what you like. It's just—it's never good to drink on your own. That's the start of the slippery slope.

Miriam What happens if you don't have the option?

Pause

Annabel Anyway, it looks corked.
Miriam What does?
Annabel The wine. It's slightly cloudy. It looks corked to me.
Miriam Tastes all right.

Pause

She's late.
Annabel Stringing us along, probably.
Miriam Possibly.

Pause

I did try, you know. I didn't just sit here vegetating. At one time, I went to
night class. Every Wednesday.
Annabel Really? What were you studying? Something useful.
Miriam Plumbing.
Annabel Plumbing?
Miriam There was a Plumbing for Women Course. But I didn't get on very
well with that. So I switched to Elementary Electrics for a bit, but that was
even more boring. I had this great idea that I could put in an extra bathroom
and re-wire the house, you see. But then Father got worse and I had to give
it all up, anyway.
Annabel Tell me, is there no-one else in your life? No-one at all?
Miriam No. Not now dear Father's gone, there isn't. No-one at all. Just this
lonely old maid. Spinster of this parish. Do you take this woman—? No,
we don't. Frightfully sorry.
Annabel What about—whoever it was…
Miriam Oh. You mean Lewis? Lewis went away. I wrote and told you.
Annabel Did you, I…
Miriam Didn't you ever read any of my letters?
Annabel Of course.
Miriam You don't appear to have done. You don't seem to know anything
about me. I read everything about you and your blessed Brad. Pages and
pages of it.
Annabel I needed to write to someone.
Miriam I could tell.

Pause

Why did you put up with it for so long? I thought you were the strong one.

Annabel It's never that simple.

Pause

I don't want to talk about it. It's over.

Miriam I don't know how you ever live with someone who hits you.

Annabel Please, I don't want to talk about it, Miriam.

Miriam Punches you in the face. How could you possibly stay with someone after that?

Annabel I didn't. I left him.

Miriam After eighteen months. You put up with it for a year, didn't you?

Annabel I've said, it's never that simple. I'm sorry, I don't want to talk about it. It's forgotten. He's gone. Out of my life. Making someone else's life a misery, no doubt. (*She laughs*)

Slight pause

(*In a rush*) And, as a result of all that, I started drinking more and more, had a mild heart attack, my business collapsed, I dried out, my sister's just killed my father and here I am home again. It's been a great life so far, hasn't it?

Pause

Maybe I'm a born loser. I don't know.

Miriam (*solemnly*) I hate people who say that. I really despise them.

Annabel (*a little startled*) What?

Miriam No-one's a born loser. (*She drinks in silence*)

Annabel I take it that—Lewis wasn't abusive?

Miriam No. Far from that.

Annabel You broke up for other reasons?

Miriam We broke up because Father didn't approve of him. He didn't like Lewis, not at all. God knows why not. But there you are. I defied him for a bit—which incidentally is probably one of the reasons I got cut out of the will… I kept on asking Lewis round despite. We never made it as far as the bedroom but at least he came round to see me. But, in the end, life was just too short. He had a very strong personality did Father.

Annabel Tell me.

Miriam Right to the end.

Annabel Why on earth didn't he like Lewis? You'd think he'd have been happy that you'd found——

Miriam Father didn't give a reason. He said he thought he was a bad influence, he didn't trust him and he didn't want him to come to the house again. It was his house, after all, what could we both do? I was tied here, we couldn't meet anywhere else much...

Annabel You could have found a way, surely?

Miriam It's never that simple.

Annabel You could always have threatened to walk out and leave him, I suppose.

Miriam (*looking at her*) We couldn't both of us do that, Annabel, could we?

Annabel (*muted*) No.

Miriam Someone has to be responsible, I think. I know you feel you were fully justified but he probably treated us both equally badly in different ways and in the end he was still our father, wasn't he?

Annabel Did he treat you badly?

Miriam Oh, you've no idea, Annabel. You really have no idea.

Annabel (*softly*) Annie.

Miriam Annie.

Pause

I think that's my greatest regret, you know. That I could so easily go to my grave having never experienced love—real love—neither having had a chance to give it nor to receive it from another human being. I can put up with all the rest of it really. No real, proper close friends, no wild social life, no nice clothes, exotic holidays, no children—I can just about cope with all that. But never to have known—never to have been able to wallow in the knowledge that you were loved by someone. Even for a second... That makes me feel very sad sometimes.

Annabel (*moved*) Oh, Miriam... (*She goes to embrace her*)

Miriam pulls away from her sharply and instinctively

Miriam Don't do that, please. That's thirty years too late, Annie. Really it is. I'm sorry.

Annabel, hurt, stares at Miriam

Annabel She was right about you, that woman. You're very different. You've changed a lot...

Miriam Yes.

Another silence between them

Alice enters from the side of the tennis court. Smartly dressed for their meeting, around her neck she wears a distinctive lightweight summer scarf. She watches them for a second

Alice 'afternoon.
Annabel (*coolly*) Good afternoon.
Miriam (*likewise*) Hallo.
Alice Another lovely day. Sitting out here then, are we? Might as well, eh?
  Take advantage of it. While we can. While it lasts. Don't often get the
  chance to, do we?
Miriam Do you want to sit down?
Alice Thank you.

Alice sits. The others sit

Miriam Would you care for a glass of wine?
Alice Oh. How nice. I hope you don't think you're going to get round me that
  way, though.
Miriam Sorry?
Alice (*amused*) You're wasting your time there, Miriam, I warn you.

Miriam pours Alice a glass of wine. Her own glass is still half full

  Ta. (*To Annabel*) You not having one?
Annabel I don't drink.
Alice Really? Doesn't know what she's missing, does she?
Annabel Yes, I do.
Alice Good health, then. (*She raises her glass to Miriam*)

Miriam drinks. Alice drinks

  Right. Lovely. Ready for our chat, are we?
Annabel Quite ready.

A silence

Alice Do I take it we have a deal, then?
Annabel That depends.
Alice On what?
Annabel On whether you're prepared to accept our offer.
Alice *Your* offer?
Annabel Yes.
Alice I don't think you've quite understood this. Your offer? I'm the one
  who's made the offer, surely. All you have to do is pay the asking price.
  Or not. That's the only choice.
Annabel We both feel that your—asking price is totally unreasonable.
Alice I see. (*She glances at Miriam*) Your sister agrees with that, does she?
Miriam —er...

Annabel Yes, she does. What you're asking is quite out of the question.
Alice I don't agree at all. I'd have thought a hundred thousand pounds is not unreasonable in return for, say, probably ten years of someone's life. Ten thousand a year—not a lot to spend for your own sister's freedom, surely?
Annabel The point is, I don't even have a hundred thousand pounds.
Alice Then you'd better find it, hadn't you?
Annabel (*irritably*) Don't be so ridiculous. Where am I going to get hold of that sort of money?
Alice I don't know. That's not my problem. You could always sell this house, I suppose. You'd get at least that much for it. Even if it is half falling down.
Annabel When I choose to sell this house, it will not be in order to give the money to you.
Miriam Yes, where are we both supposed to live, if we did that?
Alice Oh, I daresay there'd be enough change out of a hundred grand to get yourselves a nice little mobile home. Even a caravan, who knows?
Annabel A caravan?
Alice Only a small one.
Miriam We're not living in a caravan, what are you saying?
Alice Lots of people do, love.
Annabel No doubt they do. Maybe they choose to——
Alice Maybe they don't have the choice.

Silence

(*Rising impatiently*) Come on now. A hundred thousand, that's my final offer. Take it or leave it.

Alice moves away slightly

Miriam (*sotto voce to Annabel*) We can't both live in a caravan.
Annabel (*sotto voce*) Certainly not.
Miriam (*sotto voce*) We'd murder each other in a fortnight.
Annabel (*sotto voce*) Very probably.
Miriam (*sotto voce*) I mean, you've only been here twenty-four hours and you're already driving me crazy.
Annabel (*sotto voce*) I know precisely how you feel.

Alice stands near the tennis court sipping her wine

(*Trying another tack*) Listen—er… Miss…
Miriam Alice.
Annabel Alice.
Alice Made up your minds, have you?

Annabel I should tell you—I do have a heart condition.
Alice (*solicitously*) Oh, dear.
Annabel It's quite serious. I have to be—extremely careful.
Alice Well, you would, yes.
Annabel I mean, any sort of strain, you understand…
Alice (*returning to the table, sympathetically*) Yes … yes…
Annabel …could prove fatal. You see?
Alice 'dear.

Miriam refills both her own and Alice's empty glasses. Alice continues to sip hers during the following but Miriam drinks no more

Annabel And this is not—you know… All this isn't… For me. Not at all.
Alice Yes, I see.

Pause

Maybe you should try for a bungalow, then?
Annabel A what?
Alice A bungalow. A little house with no stairs, you know.
Annabel (*impatiently*) Yes, I know what a bungalow is.
Alice I mean if that's a problem for you. I do see. Even climbing in and out of a camper van could bring on palpitations, couldn't it?
Annabel (*staring at her*) I don't think you're taking me seriously, are you?
Alice (*evenly*) I don't think you're taking me seriously, either.

Silence. Annabel searches for another tack. Alice sits back at the table again

Come on then, let's hear it. How much are you prepared to offer?
Annabel (*after a slight hesitation*) Five thousand pounds.
Alice Sorry. I don't think I quite heard you.
Annabel Five thousand pounds.
Alice For the letter?
Annabel And for your promise of silence.

Pause

Alice Thanks for the wine. (*She drains her glass and makes to get up*)
Annabel What are you doing?
Alice I'm going to the police.
Miriam (*getting up as well, still clutching her glass*) No, wait!
Alice What I should have done in the first place.
Annabel Listen, two can play at that game. I can just as easily go to the police as well, you know…

Alice I should.

Annabel I'll tell them what you've been up to——

Alice Do that. I should take your sister with you. It'll save them having to come and find her.

Annabel (*angrily*) Now, look here——

Alice (*suddenly getting tough*) No, you look here, Annabel. You come up with that money or this batty little bitch of a sister of yours is going away for a very long time, all right.

Miriam's still full wine glass drops from her hand on to the grass

Miriam Oh!

Alice Whoops!

Miriam (*retrieving her glass*) Sorry...

Alice So what's your final answer going to be then, eh?

Annabel My final answer is that you're going to have to whistle, aren't you?

Alice Oh, I will, don't worry. I'll whistle. I'll whistle good and loud, I promise you that. (*She makes as if to leave again*)

Miriam Just a moment.

Alice Yes?

Miriam Please. If—we were to find the money—from somewhere— somehow—how long would you give us to raise it? How much time would you allow us?

Alice Depends, doesn't it? You're saying you think you could raise it?

Miriam Possibly.

Annabel Miriam...

Alice A hundred thousand pounds we're talking about here.

Miriam Oh, yes...

Alice And you can lay your hands on that, can you?

Miriam Probably.

Annabel Miriam, what is all this?

Alice Then what have we all been arguing about, then?

Annabel My sister doesn't know what she's saying... This is all nonsense.

Miriam (*pouring herself a fresh glass of wine*) I happen to have a friend who might be able to—lend me that much. He might—if I asked him very nicely. He's very—very fond of me. At least I think he is. (*She pours Alice a fresh glass as well*)

Annabel Who are you talking about? You don't know anyone with that sort of money. Who is this person?

Miriam His name's Lewis. You remember I mentioned him.

Annabel *Lewis?*

Miriam Lewis.

Annabel Lewis has that sort of money?

Miriam Oh, yes.

Annabel And you're saying Father didn't approve of him?

Alice Who's this you're talking about?

Miriam It's a good friend of mine called Lewis.

Alice What, him? Is this the same one who used to come round to see you when I worked here?

Miriam That's right.

Alice On his moped?

Miriam That's the one.

Alice Balding at the front with the funny haircut at the back?

Miriam That's the one.

Alice Him? He wasn't worth a fiver. He used to steal food out of your larder.

Miriam He didn't.

Alice I caught him at it. Stuffing tins of beans up his jacket.

Miriam Well, perhaps he did, occasionally. He was very eccentric.

Alice He was a bloody lunatic. No wonder your dad sent him packing. Listen, love, I'm not buying that. I'm sorry. The most you'd get out of Lewis is twenty-five quid and that's only if he sold his moped, which was probably nicked in the first place. No, I think we can safely assume that negotiations are now at an end, yes? (*To Annabel*) Am I correct?

Annabel doesn't answer

Yes?

Miriam (*anxiously*) Annabel?

Annabel (*stiffly*) Quite correct.

Alice (*draining her glass again*) Good day to you, then. See you in court, shall I? (*She puts her glass down on the table and makes to leave round the side of the tennis court*)

The others watch her, motionless

(*Turning as she goes*) I'll just say one thing, though, before I go. (*She sways slightly and slurs her speech slightly*) You've got—you've got yourself one hell of a sister there, Miriam, I have to say. When the chips are down, it's always good to feel your family's behind you, isn't it? Pres— presonally, if I had a sister like—(*swaying again*)—a sister like—a sis— what's the matter with me—a sis—is—sssss ... sssss ... sssss... (*She grabs the tennis fence in an attempt to keep upright but finally buckles at the knees and falls in a heap on the ground*)

The others watch her

Annabel What's the matter with her? What's wrong?

Miriam I think she may have had too much wine.

Annabel But she's only had—what?—three glasses…

Miriam (*moving to Alice*) Yes, but she may have had an allergy—to the—to the sediment.

Annabel It never affected you…

Miriam Oh, but I didn't drink from that one. My bottle's in the kitchen.

Annabel (*with slow realization*) Miriam! For heaven's sake—you haven't—you didn't…?

Miriam Just some pills of Father's—sedatives… (*She moves to Alice*) Help me with her, would you…? (*She begins to tug at Alice's body, trying to drag it along the ground*)

Annabel Miriam, what do you think you're doing? This is not a solution…

Miriam (*still tugging*) Help me, Annie! Are you going to help me?

Annabel All this is doing is putting off the inevitable…

Miriam Help me, please!

Annabel (*moving reluctantly over*) You can't just drug people like this, it's totally illegal…

Miriam (*slightly frenzied*) I'm not going to prison, Annie! I don't want to go to prison! I'm not going to prison. Will you help me, please!

Annabel What are we doing with her?

Miriam Over to the—over to the summer-house…

Annabel Right. Yes, that's a good idea. Then we can sit her in a chair until she recovers. Sensible idea.

Miriam Pull!

Annabel I'm pulling. (*Breathlessly*) Dear God, she's a weight.

They both begin to drag Alice towards the summer-house. Annabel is finding it heavy going. She is having increasing difficulty in breathing

Miriam Keep pulling!

Annabel (*breathlessly*) What on earth came over you? What did you hope to achieve, for heaven's sake?

Miriam Pull!

Annabel I can't do much more of this, Miriam, I really can't…

Miriam Nearly there…

Annabel No, I have to stop, I'm sorry. (*She stands panting, her hand on her chest, in some pain*)

Miriam reaches the summer-house with Alice's body

Miriam (*triumphantly*) There! (*She sees Annabel*) You all right?

Annabel (*weakly*) My bag! Would you pass my bag, please…?

Miriam Oh. Yes. (*She brings it to Annabel*) Here!

*Annabel locates her tablets and tears off another couple. Miriam removes
one of the chairs from the summer-house and places it by Annabel on the
grass*

There. You'd better sit down.
Annabel Thank you. I'll be fine. Don't worry about me. You take care of her.
   (*She sits*)
Miriam I will.

*Annabel sits, a little apart from the summer-house, hardly noticing Miriam.
She breathes deeply, taking a moment to recover from her spasm. Miriam
meanwhile is folding away the table and the garden chair to clear the trap-
door*

I mean, what was the point of drugging the woman. She's clearly quite
determined. The minute she recovers, she's going to go straight to the
police, isn't she? All you've succeeded in doing is to delay things. That's
all you've managed to do.

*During the following, Miriam pulls up the ring on the trap-door and, with
difficulty, manages to get it open. Beneath is a seemingly bottomless darkness*

(*Unaware of all this*) No, I've decided what we'll do. The best course of
action is to go to the police voluntarily ourselves, both of us together.
Before she does. Make a full confession, we needn't mention the light
bulbs—that's only her word against ours——

Miriam begins to drag the body towards the open trap-door

—and we tell them that you were in a very distressed state as a result of
nursing him day and night—with very little sleep—frayed nerves—and as
a result of that you totally miscalculated—(*She sees what Miriam is up to*)
MIRIAM! WHAT ARE YOU DOING?
Miriam Help me!
Annabel (*rising, somewhat hysterical*) What are you doing? What are you
   doing? What are you doing? (*She moves across to Miriam*)
Miriam (*heaving at the body*) Help me with her, please!
Annabel (*trying to pull the body the other way*) No!
Miriam Help me!
Annabel No!

*They have a silent tug of war over Alice for a moment or two. Annabel
eventually is forced to give up. She totters back. Miriam carries on, on her
own*

(*With difficulty*) I'm going... I'm going ... to call for help... I'm going to phone the police ... we can't do this, Miriam ... it's not right ... it's very wrong ... you see ... you must see that...

Miriam (*dragging Alice closer to the trap*) She wants me to go to prison. I'm not going to prison, Annie...

Annabel Listen, Miriam, they probably won't send you to prison at all. All they'll do, they'll probably just send you to hospital for a little bit, that's all...

Miriam Hospital? I'm not going to hospital!

Annabel Well, maybe not even hospital... Miriam, just think about what you're doing before you do it. Think very carefully. If you drop her—if you drop Alice down that well, then there is no going back, there really isn't. They certainly will put you in prison, for a very long time indeed...

Miriam now has Alice poised on the edge of the trap opening

Miriam ... think carefully. Just think very carefully now...

Miriam appears to be gathering her strength for a final effort. Alice appears suddenly to be regaining consciousness

Alice (*blearily*) What's...? What are you—? What are you? What's—?

Miriam Hyaaah! (*She topples Alice into the well*)

Annabel Miriam, no!

Alice (*receding*) Waaaahhh!

Miriam immediately slams shut the trap and stands on it

Miriam (*triumphantly*) There!

Annabel (*weakly*) Oh, no. No, no, no, no...

A moment's stillness. Annabel sits back in her chair. Miriam starts to tip away the wine glasses. She also empties the remains from the bottle into the grass

(*Incredulously*) Have you killed her?

Miriam (*quite matter-of-factly*) I imagine so. It's about thirty feet down to the water, at least. You can't even see the bottom.

Annabel Oh, God!

Miriam It was the only way, Annie. It's better this way. We're free now, you see. Both of us.

Annabel They'll find out. They're bound to find out.

Miriam How will they do that?

Annabel Because she'll be missing. Someone will miss her, Miriam. They'll come looking for her, won't they?

Miriam No, they won't. Why should they? No-one even knows she's here. She won't have told anyone. And we haven't seen her, have we? Besides, why should she want to come here, for goodness sake? (*She finds Alice's bag. She empties its contents on to the table*)

Annabel What about the letter? Father's letter?

Miriam (*sifting*) I'm just checking ... to see if she was stupid enough—or over-confident enough—to bring it with her...? No. She wasn't that stupid. But—aha—what we do have—(*she holds up an envelope*)—is her address. Not so clever. And what's the betting the letter's there?

Annabel What if it is?

Miriam We go round later on tonight, and we let ourselves in—(*she holds up some door keys*)—with her keys—and we find that original letter and then we bring it back here and we burn it.

Annabel We?

Miriam We both need to go.

Annabel Why? Why both of us?

Miriam Because you'll have to be the one that goes in there, Annie. To look for the letter. Someone might recognize me. I'm her ex-employer. It has to be you. You're unknown. A stranger.

Annabel I'm not breaking into someone's flat——

Miriam (*holding up the keys*) You don't have to. You'll have the keys. Listen, nobody knows you—and even if they saw you, you could pretend to be a friend...

Annabel I can't do that, Miriam. I'm sorry, I can't do something like that.

Miriam You're not going to help me at all, then?

Annabel Not that way. I'm sorry.

Miriam OK. You know, I believed for a moment that I might have found my sister again. But it wasn't to be, was it?

Annabel I'm sorry.

Miriam So am I. (*She tosses the keys down on the table and moves away towards the house*)

It is nearly dusk now

Annabel Wait!

Miriam stops. A pause

Whereabouts is this place?

Miriam Not far. I know the area. A ten minute drive, if that.

Annabel We could drive round there, I suppose.

Miriam All right. (*She moves back to the table and begins to scoop the contents back into Alice's handbag*)

Annabel That's if the place is not too overlooked. Then we could—I could—possibly... If it doesn't appear to be too big a risk.

Miriam (*glancing at the envelope*) It looks like a flat. From the address. Should be safe enough. (*She smiles at Annabel*) Thank you.

Annabel I haven't said I would. Yet. I said I'd take a look, that's all. Case the place. (*She laughs*)

Miriam Well, thank you, anyway. (*She gathers up the bottle and the glasses*) I'm going to rinse these out. You coming in? It's getting dark.

Annabel In a minute.

Miriam We'll have some supper first, shall we? Go round there about eleven. Late enough to avoid most people and not so late as to look suspicious. See you in a minute.

Miriam goes off to the house. She carries the bottle and glasses and has Alice's bag slung over her shoulder

Annabel, after a second, stands up again with difficulty. She takes one or two deep breaths to calm herself. She looks to the house, then moves to the trap-door. She grasps the ring and tries to open it. She struggles for some time to get it open but it is apparently too heavy for her. She stops, exhausted again. She checks in the direction of the house once more and then kneels on the floor. She knocks on the hatch

Annabel (*calling tentatively*) Hallo ... hallo ... are you all right down there? Are you still alive? Hallo... Hallo... (*She listens for a moment*)

There is no reply. She gets to her feet, moves back into the garden. She folds and tidies the chair on which she has been sitting back into the summerhouse. She is still very tense and keeps listening, as if she was hearing something. She moves towards the tennis court and looks inside. It is now sufficiently dark that she has difficulty making things out inside the court. She half turns away, as if to go to the house

A tennis ball violently and abruptly smashes into the fencing, inches from her face. Annabel screams. She backs away from the court

At the last minute, Annabel turns and rushes off towards the house

The Lights fade to Black-out

CURTAIN

ACT II

The same night. Around midnight

The garden is very dark. There is a moon but it appears to come and go. The garden chairs, the rocker and the folding table are all there as before

After a moment, from the direction of the house, two storm lanterns bob into view. These will provide the main sources of light for the remainder of the scene. The lanterns are carried by first Miriam and then, a little way behind, by Annabel. Miriam has Alice's handbag slung over her shoulder. She also swings an open bottle of wine. Both are wearing their coats

Miriam Come on, then. If you're coming.

Annabel I'm coming. I'm coming. I'm not sitting up there on my own in the dark. Why are none of the lights working all of a sudden?

Miriam I don't know. It's always happening. I told you, the whole place needs re-wiring. I had a man round to look. It'll cost a fortune. I thought of doing it myself, only... Something to do with phases and fuses, I don't know. All of a sudden they'll all go out. I'll just get rid of her bag. Now we've finished with it. Then we'll go back in and I'll light some candles.

Annabel Well, please hurry up.

Miriam Won't be long.

Annabel What about the lights out here? Don't they work either?

Miriam No, when they go, they all go off. The summer-house—even the tennis court. Amazingly, a couple of the lights in there still work as a rule. (*She clicks the switch on and off a couple of times on the summer-house column*) No. Nothing. Completely dead. (*She snaps the handle of her lantern on to a screw eye in the summer-house wall and begins struggling to open the trap*)

Annabel sits on the bench to wait. She pulls an envelope from her pocket and removing the letter inside, begins to scrutinise it by the light of her own lantern

(*Struggling with the trap-door, noticing Annabel*) Last bits of evidence. Then we can relax. Nice work, you Annie. Finding that letter. We'll burn that out here, shall we? Scatter the ashes.

Annabel (*studying the letter*) I tell you, I was terrified. Rummaging about in someone else's flat. I was convinced that at any minute someone was going to walk in on me.

Miriam Never mind. You did well. You kept your cool.

Annabel Apart from when her phone rang. Then I nearly dropped dead on the spot. Hearing the wretched woman's voice on her answering machine. (*She frowns over the letter*)

Miriam has the hatch open now. She holds the bag over the hole and then drops it, watching it fall

Miriam There you go. Down, down, down, down…

Annabel Is there any…?

Miriam What?

Annabel Sign, you know?

Miriam Of her? Not unless she's a bat with webbed feet. She'll have drowned, don't worry. She was unconscious, she won't have known a thing about it. (*About to close the trap*) Right. That's that! Unless you want a final look, yourself.

Annabel No, I do not.

Miriam Fair enough. (*She slams the trap shut and then picks up the wine bottle from the table and swigs from it*) Good night's work, eh?

Annabel (*putting away the letter*) Miriam, it has not been a good night's work. Not at all. It has been the most terrible twenty-four hours of my life. How can you say that? I don't know what it is about you. You're utterly cold-blooded.

Miriam Annie, with all the strain, the fear, the dread I've been under for the past two weeks—ever since Daddy died—ever since the accident——

Annabel Accident?

Miriam —the pressure from that woman. Her threats. This is a blessed relief, Annie. I tell you. To be free of her. Free of him. You know something? I might actually have a lie-in one morning. I might actually cook a meal when *I* want to have a meal, eat what *I* want to eat, go to bed when *I* want to go to bed. Listen to the music *I* want to listen to. Fart and swear and flush the lavatory in the middle of the night, and sing in the bath and do all the things I was meant to do but was never, never allowed to do.

Annabel If you don't mind my saying so, Miriam, those seem curiously limited ambitions.

Miriam When you've been locked in a cupboard all your life, I tell you everything can seem enormous.

Slight pause

Annabel (*coming to a decision*) Miriam, I have to tell you something.

Miriam Yes.

Annabel I don't want to alarm you, but I don't think this letter's even genuine.

Slight pause

Miriam What?

Annabel I'm sure it's almost certainly a forgery. I should have noticed it immediately but having only seen a photocopy I stupidly didn't think——

Miriam A forgery?

Annabel It's not Father's handwriting. Looking at it just now, I'm sure it isn't. Not a bad copy but even allowing for the fact that he was ill... I mean, seeing the original, it's just not his writing. I can see it now because my writing's rather similar. It's his notepaper certainly, same colour ink he used... But she would have access to all that, wouldn't she? Alice? Plenty of examples of Father's writing around for her to copy from.

Miriam (*still stunned*) It can't be. It can't be a forgery?

Annabel See for yourself. (*She hands her the envelope*)

Miriam stands by the summer-house and studies the letter by the light of her lantern. Eventually, she replaces the letter in the envelope and looks at Annabel

Well?

Miriam (*softly*) We killed her for nothing.

Annabel What are you talking about? You killed her for nothing, you mean. (*Angrily*) For God's sake, Miriam, why didn't you study that letter more closely in the first place? When the woman first showed it to you? You saw that original, didn't you? Surely you could have noticed then?

Miriam I didn't... I didn't... I panicked.

Annabel Clearly.

Miriam What are we going to do, Annie? What are we going to do?

Annabel Well, it's too late now. As you said, unless she has wings and webbed feet...

Miriam She might be still alive.

Annabel What are you talking about?

Miriam There's just a chance...

Annabel She's thirty feet down a well, Miriam.

Miriam Wait... (*She kneels by the trap and pulls it up a fraction by the ring*)

Annabel She's been there for eight hours. What are you doing?

Miriam slides her fingers under the rim of the door and gently prises it open a fraction

Miriam. It's too late! What is the point?
Miriam Sssh!
Annabel What?

They listen

Miriam (*in a whisper*) I can hear her. I think I can hear her.
Annabel (*whispering too, despite herself*) What?
Miriam I can hear her breathing down there. She's still alive. Help me!
Annabel (*gently*) Miriam, it's too late.
Miriam (*prising the trap-door further open*) Help me, Annie! Help me!

Annabel hangs back. Miriam eventually, unaided, cautiously opens the trap-door. She gazes down into the emptiness. By which time even Annabel is half expecting something or someone to emerge. Miriam, after a second, allows the trap to close again

   (*Dead*) Nothing.
Annabel It's too late, Miriam.

Silence

Miriam (*eventually*) Are you really going to sell the house? This garden?
Annabel Yes, I've said.
Miriam Why?
Annabel Because it's—impractical. I've told you.
Miriam Because it gives you the willies?
Annabel Partly that. But more important … it's just not sensible.
Miriam And you say you saw something? In the tennis court?
Annabel I—it was stupid. Probably a—probably a village boy or somesuch. Someone just hurled a tennis ball at me. It—it hit the fencing just near my face. Gave me a start, that's all.
Miriam You were outside the court?
Annabel You bet I was.
Miriam It really is a phobia for you.
Annabel It's—just I'd prefer not to go in there, that's all.
Miriam What if I came with you?
Annabel How do you mean?
Miriam Came with you and stood in the tennis court.
Annabel Don't be so silly…
Miriam I'd hold your hand. If you wanted.
Annabel What would be the point?
Miriam It's a fear. You're frightened. You need to be free from your fear, Annie. Like we all do.

Annabel I'm not frightened. I just prefer not to——
Miriam No, you're frightened.
Annabel I'm not.
Miriam Yes, you are. Don't be ashamed of it, Annie. We're all frightened
of something. We all have our secret fears. That's what sisters are for. To
help each other with their fears. You've helped me. Now I want to help you.

Pause

Go on. Say it. I'm afraid. I'm afraid.
Annabel Very well. I'm afraid. All right? Satisfied. Even though I'm aware
of the cause of it, it's still a completely irrational fear, I accept that but——
Miriam They always are. Fears. Irrational. It's because it's often to do with
things you don't know enough about. The future. Death. What's waiting
for you in the shadows? What you'll see if you open your eyes suddenly
in the night. Who it is who's standing at the foot of your bed. Who it is that's
woken you up from a deep sleep, bending over you breathing on your
cheek. Who is it moving about downstairs in that big dark empty house?
Who is it who's coming up the stairs to kiss you goodnight?
Annabel I wish you wouldn't talk like this. It's very childish.
Miriam That's because we're both still children, Annie. I'll tell you a scary
ghost story, shall I?
Annabel No, thank you.
Miriam This is really frightening. You'd left home——
Annabel Miriam, will you stop this?
Miriam You'd left home. Run off and left us all. Daddy, Auntie Gwen and
me. I was still at school, of course. Twelve years old, I must have been. And
one night there was this disco, down in the village. One or two of the kids
had—got it together. Everyone was talking about it at school. And Daddy
said, no. No, no, no, Miriam. You can't go. You're far too young. No
daughter of mine is going down there, half naked and consorting with
unsavoury village children. His actual words. Unsavoury village children.
I wonder if he'd have objected if they'd been savoury ones? Anyway, that
evening I went up to my bedroom straight after dinner, pretending I wanted
to do my homework and have an early night—but instead, I put on my
glitzy-ritzy party frock—what there was of it—lots of silver, I remember—
mostly silver—and I tossed my big party shoes out of the window on to the
grass, climbed down the drainpipe, being ever so careful not to ladder my
very naff shimmery tights and off I went to the village. Where I danced my
cares away. And I remember I was propositioned by three different boys,
all much older than me, one of whom, I recall, managed a quick grope of
my then virtually non-existent, late-developing left breast—and since
none of them I fancied in the least—I said, no thank you, that's very nice

of you but I have to go to school in the morning. And I crept back from the village. Through there, past your dreaded tennis court, a gleaming silver apparition in the moonlight, my by this time agonisingly unwearable shoes in my hand—and I saw him sitting there in that chair—(*she points to the rocking chair in the summer-house*)—Father—waiting for me. And I knew then, I was in deep trouble. And he said, you've disobeyed me, haven't you, Miriam? And I said yes. And he said, then I shall have to punish you, shan't I? You know that? And I said, yes. And he said, would you prefer to be punished here and now? And I said—I don't know what I said—I just knew it was all—wrong. Suddenly most terribly, awfully wrong. Mother should have been here, you see. You should have been here. But you weren't. Either of you. And he put me over his knee and he lifted my dress and I waited for the slap, for the sting of the pain ... but it never came. It was worse than the pain. It was worse than anything. Ever. In my whole life.

Silence

Annabel (*appalled*) Oh. Oh, Miriam.

Pause

Miriam There. Wasn't that a scary ghost story?
Annabel I had no idea.
Miriam Why should you? Just thank your lucky stars he wanted you to be a boy, that's all. All he did was hit balls at you. You got off pretty lightly, really.
Annabel Why did you never write and tell me?
Miriam I don't know. It's not something you necessarily put in a letter, is it? (*She holds out her hand*) Come on, then.
Annabel What?
Miriam Come with me.
Annabel Where are we going?
Miriam Where do you think? To face your fear. I shared mine with you. Now I want to share yours. This way. (*She pulls Annabel one-handedly towards the tennis court. In the other hand she holds her own lantern*)
Annabel (*struggling*) No, I don't want—I don't want to, Miriam...
Miriam (*gripping her fiercely*) Come on. Don't fight it now, Annie, don't fight it! Time to face your fear. Come on.
Annabel Will you let go of me, please?
Miriam Listen. You're not all that well, are you? I'm much stronger than you are. But then I've been lifting old men in and out of bed, on and off commodes, so I've built up my strength, you see. You're rather weak.

Annabel Why are you doing this?

Miriam I said, I want to share your fear, Annie. I want to feel your fear with you. Come on now, come on. Nothing's going to hurt you. It's all in your head, you see. This way. (*She opens the door of the tennis court and slowly draws the reluctant Annabel inside*)

Annabel's breathing grows heavier

There we are. There. You see. Nothing to be frightened of, is there, Annie? There.

A brief pause. Then abruptly the raucous shriek of a night bird as it flies away, startled by their presence. Annabel screams and runs from the court back to the safety of her lantern. Miriam laughs

It's only a bird, silly.

Annabel (*steadying herself with difficulty*) I'm getting very cold. Can we go indoors now, please, Miriam?

Miriam Not yet.

Annabel Please, Miriam, I need to lie down now——

Miriam Sit down...

Annabel No, I need to rest... I'm not feeling at all...

Miriam Then sit down. It's your turn.

Annabel My turn?

Miriam To tell a ghost story. It's your turn, you see. To scare me.

Annabel Oh, don't be ridiculous. I'm going indoors. I've had enough of this.

Miriam (*stepping aside*) All right.

Annabel hesitates

Off you go.

Annabel You're not coming?

Miriam In a minute I might.

Annabel Just as you like. Suit yourself. (*She takes up her lantern and with some decisiveness marches off towards the house*)

Miriam (*calling*) Mind your step, won't you? It's a bit treacherous in places, that path.

Annabel (*huffily*) I can manage.

Annabel goes off

Miriam picks up her wine bottle, takes a swig and then fetches one of the chairs down on to the grass. She stops suddenly, listening. She seems to hear something out in the darkness. In the silence, the wind chime sounds for the first time as if something had brushed past it. Miriam turns, startled

Miriam What?

The sound of Annabel returning

Annabel (*off, in some pain*) Oh, shit! Oh, bugger it!

Annabel enters angrily, limping slightly

It's locked, isn't it?
Miriam You all right?
Annabel The back door's locked.
Miriam You didn't hurt yourself?
Annabel Why didn't you tell me the bloody door was locked?
Miriam Is it? (*Vaguely*) Oh, yes. So it is.
Annabel More to the point, I found this. (*She holds out Alice's crumpled scarf*)
Miriam What is it?
Annabel What does it look like? It's hers, isn't it? It's her scarf. The woman's scarf.
Miriam (*taking it*) It can't be.
Annabel It's identical.
Miriam Where was it?
Annabel It was looped round the door handle.
Miriam It's soaking wet still. She is alive.
Annabel No, that's impossible. It's just not possible.
Miriam (*with a sudden giggle*) Maybe she does have webbed feet after all...
Annabel (*impatiently*) Miriam! If she is alive. And I suppose on this evidence we have to presume she ... she was certainly wearing that scarf when you—when she—went down there. So she's...
Miriam She could be out there. Somewhere. Possibly.
Annabel No. I can't accept that.
Miriam What do we do?

Annabel is having what appears to be the start of another attack

Annabel (*her breathing quickening*) Nevertheless, we—we would still be better off in the house, I think. She—she doesn't pose any real threat. Not any more. We know now she forged that letter, so she has no hold over you in that way whatsoever. Even if she is alive. But—but all the same...
Miriam We did drop her down a well.

Annabel No—no, let's get this straight once and for all, Miriam. You dropped her down a well. If she has a grievance at all, ration—rationally it will be with you. Not with me.

Miriam Providing she's still rational.

Slight pause

Annabel Just give me the back door key, please.

Miriam Sit down a minute. You don't look well.

Annabel I'm fine. Give me the key.

Miriam I don't want to go up there yet.

Annabel Miriam...

Miriam I heard something, just now. She may be waiting for us.

Annabel Heard? What did you hear?

Miriam She's nearby. I know she is.

Annabel Please, Miriam, come back indoors...

Miriam There's no lights there...

Annabel It's still safer than staying out here. Please.

Miriam moves to the summer-house and brings out the other garden chair

Miriam Sit down. You need to sit down a second. Look at you. (*She sets down the chair*)

Annabel I banged my leg just now, that's all. It's made me feel a bit dizzy.

Miriam Sit down, then...

Annabel (*giving in*) Well, just for a second, then. (*She sits*)

Miriam Do you need your tablets?

Annabel I'll—I'll try to do without them. I'm not supposed to take too many. Since I've been here I've been swallowing them like cough sweets. I'll be all right in a second.

Miriam sits facing her in the other chair. She swigs from her bottle

Do you think she's really out there?

Miriam I have a feeling she is. Could even be watching us.

Annabel You think so?

Miriam Maybe.

A pause. Unexpectedly, Annabel starts to cry. She does so for a moment or two whilst Miriam stares at her

Annabel (*sniffing*) Sorry. Not like me to do this. (*She cries some more*)

Miriam is motionless

I never cry. You know that. Whatever he did to me, I never cried, you know.

Miriam You mean Brad? Or Father?

Annabel Brad. Never. Maybe I should have done.

Miriam pulls a pack of tissues from her pocket and tosses them to Annabel

Miriam Here. Blow your nose, you look a mess.

Annabel Thank you. (*She blows her nose*) Sorry about that. We can go back in the house now, if you like.

Miriam (*not moving*) All right.

Annabel (*rising*) Well?

Miriam After you've told me your ghost story.

Annabel What?

Miriam I want to hear your ghost story first. (*She takes a swig from her bottle*)

Annabel What ghost story? What on earth are you talking about?

Miriam I told you mine. I want to hear yours.

Annabel Miriam, why are you doing this to me?

Miriam Sit down.

Annabel What have I done to you?

Miriam I said, sit down.

Annabel sits

That's better.

Annabel I don't understand this. Why are you being so horrible? I've done nothing to you, have I?

A fractional pause

Miriam (*softly*) What did you say?

Annabel I said—I've done nothing to you... (*She sniffs*)

Miriam That's what I thought you said. Now blow your nose and tell me a ghost story.

Annabel I don't know any bloody ghost stories. Don't be so silly...

Miriam What about Brad?

Annabel Brad?

Miriam The man who beat you. Doesn't he count as a ghost?

Annabel Hardly. He was an extremely solid one, if he was. (*She manages a laugh*)

Miriam How did you meet?

Annabel I told you.

Miriam Tell me again.

Annabel I told you everything there was to know. In my letters.

Miriam You can't have done. Tell me again.

Annabel All right. We met—at a conference. Well, one of these sales fairs, you know. I was—just starting up my business at the time, trying to get it started and he was on the next stand. His firm had the adjoining stand.

Miriam Baby clothes?

Annabel Yes. I was acting as the agent for this firm in Singapore. And Brad was—well, his firm was vast, of course. Enormous... I don't really want to go through all this again, I really don't——

Miriam Go on. You met at the sales fair. And you got talking baby wear, did you?

Annabel I think—very briefly we may have done—I think we soon got on to rather more interesting subjects by day three... (*She laughs again*)

Miriam What did you talk about, then?

Annabel Oh, I can't remember...

Miriam Try and remember...

Annabel Why on earth do you want to know? It's not important now, is it?

Miriam I need to know. I don't know you at all, you see, Annie. You walked out when I was nine and I've never seen you till now. I want to know you. I want to know about my sister. Everything.

Annabel Well, I expect you will, in due course. We're going to be talking to each other all the time, aren't we? From now on. Living together——

Miriam In Fulham...

Annabel Well, as I say possibly Fulham. We'll be sick to death of each other, I expect. Can't it wait?

Miriam I need to know now.

Annabel It's the middle of the night?

Miriam This is the best time, isn't it? The middle of the night? When it's dark. This is the time when you can let loose all those secrets you never dare normally tell. Let loose the darkness in you, so it merges with the darkness out there. This way, it never feels so bad. It's only in the daytime we're made to feel ashamed of our own darkness. Come on, Annie, tell me. What did you talk about with Brad?

Annabel We—well, we found we had things in common, of course. As people do. We enjoyed food. We used to go to restaurants a lot, I remember...

Miriam That's nice.

Annabel And, yes, we enjoyed a drink, certainly... And music. We both loved jazz. We used to go to this club, sometimes. The usual cellar, you know. I don't know why all jazz has to be played in damp cellars but there you are. And movies. We loved going to movies. The usual stuff.

Miriam What movies?

Annabel Oh. Everything. I preferred classics, you know—older movies—

black and white. Brad was more for the modern blockbusters—all those explosions—people continually shooting each other— (*She laughs*)

Miriam But you sat through them with him?

Annabel Oh, yes, well you do, don't you? If you love someone. You put up with all sorts of appalling rubbish so as not to hurt their feelings. And sooner or later—well, sooner actually—we, you know, started—sleeping together and that seemed to work out rather satisfactorily and so we— (*She laughs again. It is an increasingly nervous laugh*)

Miriam At your place?

Annabel What?

Miriam Did you sleep together at your place or his?

Annabel Oh, mostly mine. I had an impossibly small bed but at least the place was clean—his flat was quite disgusting.

Miriam Disgusting?

Annabel Well. Untidy, you know. The way men are. Usually. Most men.

Miriam Father wasn't untidy. He'd always punish you if your room was untidy.

Annabel Yes. Well, as I say, most men. Anyway, then Brad and I both decided to put things on a regular footing and we—got somewhere together. A flat. And—then got married—register office, nothing elaborate—he'd been married before, of course and—it was all fine. We were very happy. (*A slight pause*) Until one day, we both came home from work—and—he'd gone out slightly later than me that morning and he'd left the place in a bit of a mess—you know, dirty washing up, unmade beds—and I said something quite mild I think and—we were both rather tired, you understand, but he suddenly pushed me—you know—quite hard and I fell over. And that's how it started. I mean, he was terribly apologetic. Said he didn't know what had come over him—couldn't apologise enough actually—bought me flowers next day—and all that sort of thing. But it went on from there.

Miriam He would hit you?

Annabel Yes. You see the sex had gone rather—you know—as it tends to do after a bit. He started to lose interest, I think. And I began—you see this is the stupid thing—I began to try and make him notice me more. Because I still loved him, I still wanted him, you see. That way. And when he'd turn away from me in the night—I just felt so incredibly hurt. And I began to say things just to get some reaction from him—any reaction, really. But I knew—I knew exactly what I was doing, how he'd react. To the things I said. Occasionally I'd deliberately say something—quite deliberately, you know—and eventually he'd lash out—and... You see I did it deliberately. I brought it on myself. I was partly responsible for his behaviour. At least, that's how I felt at the time. And because afterwards, after he'd—hit me— he was always so remorseful, so needful for me to forgive him, so—almost

loving. Just for a while, anyway. But then even that went… And then there
was nothing. So I ran away. Again. Just another pathetic battered wife.

Miriam Why didn't you go to someone? You could have had him arrested.

Annabel Very probably.

Miriam Why didn't you?

Annabel Miriam, I was a young—youngish—dynamic businesswoman
with a suite of offices, twelve full-time employees and my own PA. Do you
realize how much pride I would have to have swallowed? I was prepared
to risk getting slapped round the face occasionally, but I wasn't brave
enough to let the world know about it. To face all those—sympathetic
looks. I was far too proud. God, I'm embarrassed enough telling you now.
You're right. Thank God, it's dark.

Miriam Did you ever enjoy it?

Annabel What?

Miriam Being hit?

Annabel What a question. Of course not. I've said, it was just part of a vicious
cycle. I certainly didn't enjoy it. Nobody likes being hit.

A slight pause

Don't tell me you did? I mean when Father punished you, you didn't enjoy
that, surely?

Miriam I don't know now. Sometimes anything is better than being left
alone, isn't it?

Slight pause

When you think about it. It's all tied in with love really, isn't it? Love's at
the root of everything. Or what we believe to be love. What we understand
as love. Father—he used to shout at us, he used to smack us, because he
loved us. Or that's what he believed. I'm doing this for your own good, he
used to say. Because I love you, Miriam. And Brad, he probably hit you
because he loved you.

Annabel Yes?

Miriam Yes, because he cared. He cared what you thought about him. If he
didn't care about you at all, he would never have touched you, would he?
I mean he didn't go around slapping strangers in the street, did he? Did he
ever pick fights in pubs?

Annabel Not as far as I know.

Miriam Of course not. Only you. He only hit you. You were the only one
that mattered enough. Unless we're mad or deranged those are the only
people we ever try to hurt. The people we love. The people we need to love
us. People who've somehow taken their love away from us. Spurned our
love. Left us on our own. Those are the ones we want to hurt.

Annabel (*uneasily*) Yes. Well, was that enough of a ghost story for you? Can we go inside now, please?

Miriam It was a terrific ghost story, Annie. Thank you. But the point is, do you feel better for telling it?

Annabel I—maybe. Maybe, maybe I do.

Miriam (*kneeling at Annabel's feet, softly*) That's why I'm your sister. That's why I'm here, Annie. (*She kisses Annabel's hands*) I love you.

Annabel (*uneasily*) Miriam, let's go in, now.

Miriam Sure.

Quite suddenly the lamp nearest them, Annabel's, flickers and dies. Only the one in the summer-house now remains alight

Annabel Oh, no!

Miriam (*springing up*) It's OK. It's out of oil. Hang on! Wait there!

Annabel Where are you going?

Miriam To fetch a torch. Back in a second.

Annabel We've still got the other lamp, why can't we take that one?

Miriam Because that'll run out in a minute. Bound to. Won't be a sec.

Annabel But we can both use the...

But Miriam has disappeared into the darkness, back towards the house

Oh, for heaven's sake! (*She hesitates*) Well, I'm not sitting out here on my own, I can tell you that. (*She moves to unfasten the other lamp from the screw eye in the summer-house wall. She fiddles irritably with it for a second but can't figure how to release it*) Dammit. Wretched thing! (*She stands back and stares at the lantern in frustration*)

As she does this, it also flickers and goes out. Annabel is now alone in virtual darkness

Oh, for God's sake!! Miriam! Miriam! Oh, no... (*She gropes in the darkness in what she hopes is the direction of the house. She can evidently see nothing. She trips over one of the chairs and cries out. She is breathing heavily again*) Oh, bugger! Miriam! (*Yelling*) Miriam! (*To herself*) I can't even find my bag. (*She gets on to her hands and knees*) Where's my bloody bag? (*She gropes about on the grass but fails to find it. She starts to panic*) Oh, this is hopeless. (*She takes deep breaths*) Keep calm. Keep calm. She'll be back in a minute. (*She waits, kneeling on the ground. To herself*) Come on! Come on, Miriam! Where are you, woman?

Suddenly, in the darkness, something clangs against the tennis court fence. It's another tennis ball

What's that? Who's there? (*She listens*) Who is that? Miriam? Who's in there?

From the other end of the court, a man's voice is heard calling softly

Man (*off, in all but a whisper*) Annabel... Annabel...
Annabel (*rising to her feet*) What?
Man (*off*) Annabel...
Annabel (*incredulously*) Father? *Father?*
Man (*off*) Annabel...
Annabel Listen, who is this? Come out of there, do you hear me? You come out this minute! You're not frightening me. Come on. (*She moves tentatively towards the tennis court. Her fingers make contact with the mesh*) You come out, do you hear? Or I'm coming in. I say, I'm not frightened of you. Come on! Come out at once! (*She pushes the gate slowly open*) I'm coming in, do you hear? (*She cautiously enters the tennis court*)

Just the sound of her breathing, quite laboured now. She stands inside the court listening intently

Where are you? I know you're in here.

The gate behind her slams shut violently. She turns with a cry and tries to open it but she has difficulty in the darkness locating the handle. All at once a brilliant light shines from the other end of the court. Annabel, turning to look, is blinded by it. Simultaneously, the man's voice is heard, very much louder now

Man (*off; loudly*) Annabel...! Annabel...! Annabel...! Annabel...! Annabel...! Annabel!

Tennis balls come hurtling down the court in rapid succession, some hitting the fencing, the occasional one hitting Annabel. Annabel whimpers in terror and fumbles for the catch on the gate. At last she finds it and manages to escape from the court. As she does so, abruptly the voice, the tennis balls stop and the light goes out. Annabel stands moaning to herself in the darkness

Annabel Help me, please! Dear God, somebody help me! Please!

From the summer-house the sound of someone scrabbling at the trap-door. Annabel stands frozen in horror. The trap lid is raised slowly

First a hand, then the face and head and shoulders of Alice as she emerges filthy, bedraggled and bloody

Annabel, transfixed by this apparition, begins to retreat. Her breathing has now become a series of wheezing rasps. As she backs away, she finally makes contact again with the tennis court fence. She slithers slowly down till she is sitting upright, propped against it. Her body gives a final couple of convulsions, goes rigid and she is suddenly very still, her eyes closed. Alice climbs out of the trap-door and walks over to Annabel. She spends a moment checking her pulse for signs of life

Soon Miriam emerges from the far end of the court. She carries a ghetto blaster

Alice (*still busy with Annabel*) I thought you said she had a weak heart?
Miriam She had.
Alice She was as strong as a bloody ox.
Miriam But she's——
Alice Oh, yes. Don't worry, she's dead now. (*She moves back to the trap and makes to close it*)
Miriam (*staring at Annabel*) Should we put her in a chair or something?
Alice No! Don't move her. Leave everything as it is. Just make sure the tennis court is clear.
Miriam Yes, I will.

Alice, remembering something, steps back into the hole. It is now revealed as not being very deep at all. She retrieves a half empty plastic bottle of water

Alice It's a bloody good job we had this filled in. The way you dropped me this afternoon, I could have broken my neck. (*She steps out of the hole and closes the trap*)
Miriam It needed to look convincing.
Alice All right, are you?
Miriam Yes, I just—keep thinking there's—something … nearly seeing things.
Alice You've frightened yourself, that's all.
Miriam Probably. (*She giggles a little nervously*)

Alice grabs Miriam's wrists and pulls her to her

Alice (*gently*) Well done, little Mir, you did well, girl. (*She kisses Miriam gently on the lips*)
Miriam (*smiling*) Well done yourself, Lewis.
Alice (*mock aggressively*) Lewis! I'll give you Lewis… (*She releases her*) What's the time, anyway?

Miriam produces a small pocket torch and shines it on her wrist-watch

Miriam Just gone twenty past two.

Alice Twenty past *two*? This was supposed to be over by midnight, wasn't it?

Miriam It took longer than I thought.

Alice You any idea how long I've been down that bloody hole. Three hours.

Miriam I'm sorry…

Alice Sort you out later, won't I?

Miriam giggles

I need to get washed up. Get all this muck off.

Miriam I'll tidy up here.

Alice Don't touch her, will you. Leave her there exactly as she is till the morning. You get up at your normal time, see her bed's not been slept in, so when you find she's not in the house, you come down here looking for her, all right? Then you make the phone call.

Miriam Yes. I know…

Alice (*standing over Miriam*) She must have gone for a walk in the middle of the night. Had an attack. How sad.

Miriam Very sad.

Alice See you in a minute, then.

Miriam (*handing Alice the torch*) Here. Back door key's in the usual place.

Alice (*moving off*) Ta! It's all ours now, isn't it? All ours, eh?

Miriam Yes. (*In a murmur*) All mine. (*She calls*) Alice!

Alice Yes?

Miriam When you get in, could you put the lights on again? So I can see what I'm doing. You know where it all switches on, don't you? In the basement.

Alice Sure.

Miriam Watch your step, though. There's a lot of water on the floor down there, for some reason. I think we must have had a leak.

Alice Bloody house. Sooner we sell it the better. (*She laughs as she goes*) Lewis! Where the hell'd you get Lewis, then?

Alice goes off

Miriam starts to tidy up. She replaces the chairs in the summer-house and picks up Annabel's bag and puts it closer to her body, as if she had dropped it when she collapsed. She kisses Annabel on the forehead

Miriam Goodbye, dear sister…

Momentarily, both the mains lights in the summer-house and the lights in the tennis court come on. It is briefly very bright. Just as suddenly all the lights flicker a couple of times and then go out again

(*Looking towards the house*) Whoops. Bye-bye, Lewis.

Miriam continues with her tasks, placing the ghetto blaster and the wine bottle ready to take back to the house. She takes another swallow from the wine bottle as she does this. She now turns her attention to the tennis court. She pauses for a moment to remove her coat which she tosses on to the bench. Underneath she is wearing a silver party dress. It is quite old—designed for a young teenager rather than for a woman of Miriam's age. It is consequently rather tight fitting and looks somewhat incongruous. She goes into the tennis court where she starts to gather up the balls that have accumulated along the fence, rolling them back to the other end of the court. The lantern in the summer-house suddenly flickers into life. Miriam turns, startled, and stares. The wind chime again tinkles briefly. Miriam moves cautiously to the doorway of the court. Slowly the rocking chair starts to move gently to and fro as if someone was sitting there. Miriam stands transfixed. Whoever it is in the chair, she alone can see them. The man's voice is again heard, softly from the summer-house

Man (*softly*) Miriam… Miriam…

Miriam is now motionless

Miriam (*in horror, softly at first*) Father…? Father…? (*With a scream of sheer terror*) FATHER, NO!!

Still slumped against the fencing where she fell, Annabel's eyes open in a final deathly stare

The Lights fade to Black-out

CURTAIN

FURNITURE AND PROPERTY LIST

Further dressing may be added at the director's discretion

ACT I

SCENE 1

On stage: Tennis court with fencing and door
Bench
Summer-house/pavilion containing rocking chair and wind chime
Trap door
Rough grass
Bushes and trees

Off stage: Bag containing sheet of paper (**Alice**)

Personal: **Miriam**: wrist-watch (worn throughout)

SCENE 2

Set: **Annabel**'s handbag containing strip of tablets

Off stage: Small folding table, upright garden chair (**Miriam**)
Tray with depleted bottle of white wine and three glasses, one already filled (**Miriam**)
Glass, second folding chair (**Miriam**)
Shoulder bag containing envelope and door keys (**Alice**)
Tennis ball (**ASM**)

ACT II

Set: Half empty plastic bottle of water in well hole

Off stage: 2 storm lanterns (**Miriam** and **Annabel**)
Alice's handbag, open bottle of wine (**Miriam**)

        Alice's crumpled scarf (**Annabel**)
        Tennis balls (**ASM**)
        Ghetto blaster (**Miriam**)

Personal: **Annabel:** letter in envelope
        Miriam: pack of tissues, small pocket torch

LIGHTING PLOT

Practical fittings required: 2 storm lanterns
1 exterior. The same throughout

ACT I, Scene 1

To open: Late afternoon in August

Cue 1 **Miriam**: "…sure to think of something." (Page 11)
Fade lights to black-out

ACT I, Scene 2

To open: Very warm and sunny, slowly fading to dusk

Cue 2 **Miriam** moves away towards house (Page 30)
Continue fading to dusk

Cue 3 **Annabel** turns and rushes off (Page 31)
Fade lights to black-out

ACT II

To open: Very dark with varying moonlight

Cue 4 **Annabel** and **Miriam** bring on lanterns (Page 32)
Back up lanterns

Cue 5 **Annabel** goes (Page 38)
*Cut back up to **Annabel**'s lantern*

Cue 6 **Annabel** returns (Page 39)
Back up lantern

| *Cue* 7 | **Miriam**: "Sure." | (Page 45) |
| | *Flicker and turn off* **Annabel***'s lantern and backup* | |

| *Cue* 8 | **Annabel** stares at **Miriam**'s lantern | (Page 45) |
| | *Flicker and turn off* **Miriam***'s lantern and backup* | |

| *Cue* 9 | **Annabel** tries opening the gate | (Page 46) |
| | *Shine brilliant light from other end of court* | |

| *Cue* 10 | **Annabel** escapes from court | (Page 46) |
| | *Turn off brilliant light* | |

| *Cue* 11 | **Miriam**: "Goodbye, dear sister…" | (Page 48) |
| | *Bring up mains lights in summer-house and lights in tennis court, flicker twice, snap off* | |

| *Cue* 12 | **Miriam** rolls tennis balls to other end of court | (Page 49) |
| | *Flicker lantern in summer house into life* | |

| *Cue* 13 | **Annabel**'s eyes open | (Page 49) |
| | *Fade lights to black-out* | |

EFFECTS PLOT

ACT I

Cue 1	To open Scene 1 *Cheerful birdsong*	(Page 1)
Cue 2	**Miriam**: "A hundred thousand pounds." *Silence, end birdsong*	(Page 10)

ACT II

Cue 3	**Miriam**: "…is there, Annie? There." *After brief pause, shriek of night bird as it flies away*	(Page 38)
Cue 4	**Annabel**: "Who's in there?" **Man***'s voice on tape from other end of court as script page 46*	(Page 46)
Cue 5	**Annabel** escapes from court *Cut* **Man***'s voice*	(Page 46)
Cue 6	**Miriam** turns and stares *Make wind chime tinkle briefly*	(Page 49)
Cue 7	Rocking chair starts rocking **Man***'s voice on tape from summer-house as script page 49*	(Page 49)

MADE AND PRINTED IN GREAT BRITAIN BY
LATIMER TREND & COMPANY LTD PLYMOUTH
MADE IN ENGLAND